The author was born in Tickhill Yorkshire in 1948. He is very proud of his Yorkshire roots. He still works full time employed as a painter decorator for a large construction company in Doncaster. David has two sons and a daughter to his first wife, and is also a grandad and great grandad. He is now very happily married to his second wife, and they love to watch darts, rugby league and union and soccer; Leeds United are his team (followed since 1967).

Malin

FEELINGS

AUSTIN MACAULEY PUBLISHERS™
LONDON • CAMBRIDGE • NEW YORK • SHARJAH

Copyright © Malin 2024

The right of Malin to be identified as author of this work has been asserted by the author in accordance with sections 77 and 78 of the Copyright, Designs and Patents Act 1988.

All rights reserved. No part of this publication may be reproduced, stored in a retrieval system, or transmitted in any form or by any means, electronic, mechanical, photocopying, recording, or otherwise, without the prior permission of the publishers.

Any person who commits any unauthorised act in relation to this publication may be liable to criminal prosecution and civil claims for damages.

A CIP catalogue record for this title is available from the British Library.

ISBN 9781035844616 (Paperback)
ISBN 9781035844623 (Hardback)
ISBN 9781035844630 (ePub e-book)

www.austinmacauley.com

First Published 2024
Austin Macauley Publishers Ltd®
1 Canada Square
Canary Wharf
London
E14 5AA

I would like to thank Austin Macauley Publishers for giving me the platform to bring you my work and allowing me to bring you tributes, love, hope, inspiration and truth.

World	30
Ivory	31
Memories	32
Three wishes	33
Princess of love	34
You	35
Your love	36
Rock on	37
Dawn	38
On the streets	39
Your future	40
When I leave	41
Passion	42
Beauty	43
Spring Love	44
Destruction	45
Lonely heart	46
Time	47
No love	48

Table of Contents

Poetry 9

Our beloved queen 10

Mother 11

Princess Diana 12

Our Princess of Hearts 13

Tribute 14

Tom 15

The Tyrant 16

Pollution 17

Suicide 18

Sleep of Death 19

Doomsday 20

Darkness 21

Life 22

Millenium dawn 23

Age 24

Climax 25

First Christmas 26

Savior 27

Yorkshire 28

Heaven 29

Poetry

The gift of writing poetry
Is a very special art,
To give it deepest feeling
You must write from the heart.

Love of life is crucial
To help you write this way,
Have faith in what you write about,
Believe in what you say.

Words bring joy and pleasure
Tears and sadness too,
Words have special meanings
These words I bring to you

Our Beloved Queen

Countless tears have fallen
We share our loss and pain,
Our beloved Queen in heaven
But her love will still remain.

In a long and glorious reign
Our Queen gave the world her love,
Now with a host of angels
Our Queen will guide us from above.

Our Princess of Hearts

The princess of all our hearts
Is now laid to rest,
A friend who cared, a mother,
Princess Diana was the best.

May the princess now find lasting peace,
In heaven may she sleep,
Our princess gave such love and care,
Fond memories of her we keep.

Our princess of all beauty
An angel so divine,
A miracle from heaven
Her looks were so refine.

She was the one with pure charm
For all the world to view,
A treasure sent from paradise
Princess Diana…we still love you.

Tribute

Hell came on that morning
Brought anger grief and pain,
We remember in our prayers
The victims in Dunblane.

Please God save the tears we shed
They must not fall in vain,
Let them form a sea of love
For the families of Dunblane.

Tom

With a heart as big as Yorkshire
And with covid virus rife,
Tom walked the walk for angels
As they fight to save a life,
With all our frontline heroes
And as Tom's feet walk the floor,
We will beat this evil virus,
Arise Tom 'Ilkley' Moore.
Sir Tom is now in heaven,
But in our darkest days
He gave hope and inspiration,
For this we give him praise.

The Tyrant

The tyrant rapes and plunders
This land he does not own,
His armies all seem brainwashed,
An evil seed is sown.

A brilliant army is amassed
To keep the foe at bay,
His army get well beaten
They turn and run away.

We think that war is over
That we have peace at last,
But the tyrants sends his army out
Innocents they blast.

Other countries go to help
To feed and clothe each day,
But as another baby dies
The tyrant gets away.

Pollution

Our planet once so beautiful
This earth that was so fair
Is being destroyed by greedy men
But they don't seem to care.

With acid in the rain clouds
And sewage in the seas,
Toxic waste is everywhere
It's even in the trees.

We must stop this pollution
Return to clear blue skies,
Think of life and nature
Before our planet dies.

Suicide

He waited for her patiently
But she never came,
She stood him up for someone new
Heartbroken once again.

The music was still playing,
His meal remained untouched,
He knew they would not meet again
Hurt can cause so much.

His house looked very eerie
No lights were on inside,
An empty bottle in his hand…
A tragic suicide.

Sleep of Death

The sleep of death eternal
From this you do not wake,
No movement from your body
When death your life does take.

In death your heart stops beating
Your eyes no longer see,
Life is all drained from you
Your spirit is set free.

Death will surely happen
When fate gives the call,
The only certain thing in life
Death happens to us all.

Just pray you go to heaven
When your life does cease,
To dwell with all the angels
And find eternal peace.

Doomsday

Darkness falls upon the planet
Our Earth about to die,
Out of space come aliens
Marauders from the sky.

Spaceships firing their weapons
Destroying all they see,
Aliens we are told do not exist
Yet what else could these be.

Ignoring all the sightings
So many facts could not be lies,
Counting down to doomsday
Obliteration from the skies.

Mankind wiped out forever
Immortalized in verse,
Now our planet Earth destroyed
Gone from the universe.

Darkness

I wonder where the light goes
When I see the darkness falling,
Only darkness holds the secret,
Will there be another dawning?

Will the darkness take me
On a journey far away,
Will I awake from darkness
To see the light of day?

Only darkness holds the answers
In the circle of unknown
Will I return to darkness
As from darkness I have grown

Life

Life is what you make it
So just give it a try,
A very special service
But sometimes makes you cry.

When you lose someone special
Or a loved one goes away
Life takes a lot of effort
But should get easier each day.

Do not feel downhearted,
Try to stand up tall,
Learn to live life to the full,
Life happens to us all.

Millenium Dawn

Time for all to celebrate
On a new millennium dawn,
As we plan for our future
New technology is born,
Exploring deeper into space
It may happen very soon,
Let Earth become pollution free
Life and Earth need this protection,
End of terminal illness
New drugs to fight infection,
Nuclear war could happen
If the tyrant gets his way,
Unite to beat the tyrant
Madness must not win the day,
Dawn of the new millennium
A new path for all to follow,
Walk it wise and safely
New hope…a new tomorrow.

Age

Do not worry over age
For age is just a number,
Age is only in the mind
So just let old age slumber.

Thinking younger within your mind
Will bring a special glow,
Do not count age let it be,
Just go with the flow.

You may meet someone younger,
And if love should play a part
Age difference is just a number,
But love is from the heart.

So keep a young and open mind
Youthful always be,
Age is a time of numbers
So let your age run free.

Climax

As I awake from sleeping
I feel your body close to mine,
Touching skin as soft as velvet
Is a feeling so divine.

Your bosom soft and tender
Against my naked chest,
As newborn babes together
Brings a passion filled with zest.

We kiss and pulses quicken
As sensual feelings soar,
The climax in life together
Is the ultimate sexual score.

We will be in paradise
Eternal feelings give,
Destiny will bless our love
Sincere this love we live.

First Christmas

The stars shone down on Bethlehem
As in a cattle stall,
Mother Mary bore a child
The savior for us all.

Three wise men to the stable came
Arriving from afar,
They came in search of Jesus
Guided by a brilliant star.

Shepherds left the flock to sleep
Told they would not stray,
Then shown the way by angels
On that first Christmas day.

The wise men brought gifts of riches,
Shepherds brought their love,
Angels sang their praises
For the baby from above

Savior

God sacrificed his only son
To take our sins away,
We remember this at Easter
When we kneel to pray.

Ignorant men took Jesus
They nailed him to a cross
Crucified the Son of God
This act was their loss.

Jesus arose to save us
To guide us on our way,
The Son of God is with us
To listen when we pray.

Yorkshire

Of all the Shires in England
One stands out from the rest,
God's own county Yorkshire
This Shire is the very best.

Proud to be from Yorkshire
Yorkshire born and bred,
To wear with pride on Yorkshire Day
A rose of white…not red.

The stillness of the Yorkshire Moors
The bustle of the town,
Yorkshire is the place to be,
The jewel in England's crown.

Heaven

There is a place called Heaven
May I go there when I die,
A very peaceful resting place
Where I never need to cry.

After all the stress in life
The love, the hate and pain
May Heaven be my dwelling place
Till I am born again.

The good times and the bad times
They have all gone by,
Heaven is the place for me
Where all the angels fly.

World

Why does the world keep turning
This thought keeps passing by,
Our world must keep on going round
So we can laugh and cry.

But now the ozone layer is dying
The rain forests soon will be gone,
Man is helping destroy our world
The world that life depends upon.

When our world stops revolving,
The birds no longer sing,
Our universe will fade away,
The end of everything.

Ivory

The evil ivory poachers
Leave bodies in their wake,
Carrying out this evil deed
Atrocious facts they make.

The cost of ivory is high
And heartless poaching rife,
The price paid by the animal
The precious gift of life.

Killing for greed and pleasure
This is not a sport,
Let the poacher face the gun
As a last resort.

Memories

Memory is a gift we hold
Bringing happiness or pain,
Life is filled with memories
And with us they remain.

Remembering a first date,
Your baby's first breath of air,
Fonds memories to treasure
Filled with love and care.

Memories sometimes make us cry
But with these we cannot part,
Fond memories of a loved one
Bring feelings from the heart.

Three Wishes

If I could have three wishes
This is what they would be,
To have, to hold, forever
Your beauty close to me.

To have you ever present,
Hold you in my arms,
And be in love forever
With someone with your charms.

Happy hours spent together
Bring deep love from inside,
Such passion and emotion felt
When you are by my side

Princess of love

Fortunate to meet you,
An angel from above,
Natural is your beauty
The princess of all love.

Attractive and so sexy
Sending out a sensual feeling,
To see you any time of day
It sends my senses reeling.

Charisma oozes from you,
I sense a passionate zest
Sincere feelings from within
Neath and beating breast.

I see eyes that hypnotize,
Charm straight from the heart,
Kissable lips so tender
Infatuated from the start.

You

You made the storm blow over
The sun begin to shine,
A very special person
So grateful you are mine

I will never hurt you
You will never need to cry,
My love will last forever
Yours till the day I die

Every time is see you
I fall deeper into love,
My prayers have all been answered
Your love sent from heaven above.

Your Love

You are the sun that shines on me
The breeze that blows my hair,
You are the breath I breath inside
So please take special care.

With your heart of an angel
And the wings of a dove,
God answered my prayers
With the gift of your love.

Cupid shot an arrow
Straight into your heart,
Bonding us together
So we never ever part.

Rock On

Mates we will be forever
After all we have been through,
Remembering the outdoor gigs
Knebworth and Donington too.

Alcohol and heavy rock
No regrets at all,
Shaking heads to the music
And drinking till we fall.

Numerous rock bands we have seen
Drunk a few pints too,
Remember I will not forget
A rocking mate like you.

Dawn

Dawn is the beginning
Needed to guide the way,
With us till the end of time
Dawn brings light of day.

Dawn could bring a sweet romance
A love that will not die,
When dawn brings a love so true
No dawn will make you cry.

Dawn brings a daytime challenge,
Dawn is special in every way,
Without dawn life would not exist,
No dawn would mean no day.

On The Streets

Discarded by society
Street life is all they know,
Sleeping in a cardboard box
They have nowhere else to go.

In the bitter cold of winter
Will they survive another night,
Find the homeless shelter
We must end their awful plight.

The life gone from her body
On that freezing winter night,
Just sixteen and sleeping rough
No shelter was in sight.

The homeless they are human too
We must show them that we care,
Bring them in out of the cold
They must not die out there.

Your Future

Forget about mistakes you made
And learn to look ahead,
Make the best use of your life
You are a long time dead.

So think about your future
Have faith in what you do,
Go out and give life your best shot
Your future lies with you.

Follow your own judgement,
Let your future flow,
Taking good and bad in life
In stature you will grow.

When I Leave

When my life is over God
Please bless those I leave,
Comfort those who cry for me
Take the hurt from those who grieve.

Thankful for my lifetime
I have been good and bad,
Not always doing what I should
But for life I have been glad.

My dear family and friends
I lived life to the full,
Just like Bon Jovi keep the faith
Then your life will not be dull.

Think of the happy times we shared,
My love will stay forever true,
Although you cannot see me
I will always be with you.

Passion

Your presence is exciting
Dreams in life we share,
Electric is our romance
Love making everywhere.

Nothing stops your red-hot passion
Sensual feelings they rise too,
Erotic action just takes over
X-Rated in the ladies loo.

Red-hot nights of action
Bring erotic ecstasy,
Bodies blended into one
Sexual feelings are set free.

Beauty

Your lips as red as roses
Skin so soft and fair,
You are a stunning masterpiece
Adorned with loving care.

Your beauty like a rainbow
A living jewel to behold,
You are a precious treasure
With a heart of pure gold.

God's gift of creation
With such a sweet angelic face,
Excited by your presence
None could take your place.

Spring Love

When you meet someone special
Then love becomes like Spring,
The freshness of wild flowers
Make your heart want to sing.

Lambs frisk in the meadow
The doves coo in the trees,
Beauty blooms around you
In a passionate spring breeze

The songbirds sweetly singing
Fly in the sky so blue
Precious gifts of nature
Sent from heaven just like you.

Destruction

Just to test a nuclear bomb
Our earth is blown apart
The destruction must be stopped
Let sense rule the heart.

You wonder why the earth quakes
And why our earth keeps breaking
Earth is only giving back
The damage man is making.

Countries blown apart in war
Greed destroys the living,
Tyrants must not win the day
Stop !! the damage they are giving.

Lonely Heart

Life can be so lonely
When your life has no romance,
You ask yourself this question
Will I get another chance?

A true romance is special
Through cupid you will meet,
Until that day is realized
Alone your heart must beat.

But romance is not everything
Family and friends are always near,
Let your lonely heart keep beating
Giving love to those held dear.

Time

From a time before creation
To a time of Mother Earth,
Into a time of timeless wonder
To a time that gives us birth.

Time signals springtime freshness
The summer sun to glow,
Russet leaves to fall in autumn
Before the winter snow.

Will time bring a romance,
Or will time let love go by,
Time can bring such happiness
Time can make us cry.

Time can help to ease our pain
But will time help us to forgive,
Solutions only found in time
Because in time we live.

Will time last forever
Time has gone by is now, or due,
Each span of life is a lifetime
But in time…time runs out too.

No Love

She did not feel as he did
It hurt to hear her say
I will never love you
Then she turned and walked away.

Her beauty gone forever,
No love left in his life,
His broken heart is bleeding
As if stabbed by a knife.

He drank to drown his sorrows
Drinking in his favourite bar,
This did not heal his broken heart,
He died in a fume filled car.

Made in the USA
Monee, IL
03 May 2026